THE STORY OF
William
WALLACE

D0046174

CORBIE

Text by David Ross
Illustrated by Janek Matysiak

© 1998 Waverley Books Ltd
Reprinted 1999, 2001, 2002, 2003, 2004, 2006

Published by Waverley Books Ltd,
New Lanark, Scotland

ISBN 10: 1 902407 06 7
ISBN 13: 978 1 902407 06 7

Printed and bound in UAE

THE STORY OF
WILLIAM WALLACE

This story happened seven hundred years ago
in Scotland.

A young man had been out fishing in the river near his home. He caught several fish and put them in his basket to take back. As he walked home again, a group of men stopped him.

"Hey, you. We'll have those fish," they said.

They were English soldiers. In those days, Scotland and England were two separate countries, but King Edward of England claimed that he was the overlord of Scotland. When King John of Scotland would not do what Edward wanted, Edward came to Scotland with an army and took John away to prison in London. Now Scotland was left with no king. Edward was the ruler, and he put his own governors in charge. English soldiers were placed throughout the country to watch over the people of Scotland. The Scots were angry, but most of them were also afraid. Anyone who annoyed the English would be put in prison, beaten or killed.

"You can have some of my fish," said the young man.

"We'll have it all," they said, and one of them tried to grab the basket.

"Oh no, you won't!" The young man raised his fishing rod and struck the soldier's arm away. Then

he drew his sword. At this the soldiers fled away, and he went on home with his basket of fish.

Here is another story about the same young man.

It was market day in the little town of Lanark, and the country people had come in from the farms around about to sell their produce to the townsfolk. Merchants set up their stalls by the town cross to sell clothes, knives, spice and wine. Tinkers came to mend pots. Fortune tellers and beggars joined the crowd. It was a busy day.

The market crowd was watched by English soldiers. Into the market place of Lanark walked our young man. He was very tall, wearing a green coat, and he stood out in the crowd. People seemed to know him well, and some went up and talked to him. Others moved away, looking in fear at the English soldiers.

"Who is that man?" a soldier asked one of the passers-by.

"His name is Wallace, William Wallace, your honour. That's all I know." The man hurried away.

Soon there was a little crowd round the tall young man. Laughter rose up. Children gathered round. As the English soldiers looked on, one little boy put his hand behind his back and waggled his fingers. They knew what that meant. When the Scots wanted to annoy the English, they

9

pretended that English people had tails hidden under their clothes. This was enough to send the soldiers angrily forward to break up the crowd. One of them made a grab for the boy.

"Leave him," said the tall young man. His hand was on the hilt of his long sword.

"Who might you be to give us orders?" demanded the soldier. He made a snatch for the young man's sword. With a clash of steel, the long sword was drawn and the soldier fell back. The little boy fled, and so did the townspeople and the stall-holders. Now only William Wallace was left facing the soldiers. They were too many for him. Sword in hand, he ran down the street, dodged into a side street and knocked on the door of a woman he knew. She let him in.

In a moment the soldiers were hammering at the door. The woman had barred it and pretended that she could not open it again. In the end the Englishmen broke the door down and rushed into the house. But by then William Wallace had vanished through the back door and was in the safety of the woods outside the town.

King Edward's chief man in Lanark was Sheriff Hazelrigg. It was his job to keep people in order. He arrested the woman who had rescued Wallace and had her put to death. The townspeople were horrified but could do nothing to prevent it.

When Wallace heard of what had happened, he came to Lanark that very night. With a band of friends he made his way to the sheriff's house.

"Who is that?" called the sheriff as he heard hammering at his door.

"William Wallace, whom you would slay," came a voice from outside. In a moment the door was broken through. A minute later Sheriff Hazelrigg was dead, slain by Wallace's great sword.

To kill King Edward's sheriff was as bad as

striking against the king himself. Wallace was immediately an outlaw. He could not return to his father's house at Elderslie. Every English soldier in the area was searching for him. He had to move about in secret. But he and his men knew all the ways and secret places in the thick forests. There were many meetings among the trees. Messengers from Wallace's hiding place travelled all over Scotland, unknown to the English governors. The bishops of the Scottish church, especially the rich and powerful bishop of Glasgow, supported him. For Wallace was no common outlaw. He had a dream. He wanted to see the English driven out of Scotland and to bring back the Scottish king. He knew that many people shared his dream. But Wallace was not just a dreamer. He was a man of action.

With a larger band of followers, he struck again. This time it was at the great abbey of Scone, where Ormsby, one of the chief English officers, was based. The officer fled to safety, but Wallace captured a large amount of treasure and baggage.

By now the name of William Wallace had reached London. King Edward had believed that Scotland was firmly under his control. Now he learned that from all over the country men were hurrying to join Wallace. The young man in green no longer had a small band of followers. He had an army. And his example inspired others. One of these was a young nobleman, Robert Bruce, the Earl of Carrick in Ayrshire. Another was Andrew Murray, who came from Moray in the northeast.

But the day when Bruce would become King Robert and finish the task that Wallace began was still far off. When Bruce's army was faced by a small English army at Irvine, it ran away. Andrew Murray did far better, capturing castles in the north and raising many men to help in the fight. Then he joined up with Wallace. They were named as the two Guardians of Scotland. Soon, they knew, a great English army would come to regain control of Scotland. King Edward of England was not a man to give up.

When the English army did come, they were ready to meet it. At the Battle of Stirling Bridge, Wallace and Murray defeated a great English force. In fact, not all the men on the English side were Englishmen. Some of the Scottish lords had decided to follow Edward. He had promised them more land and power if they would support him. Their men had to fight against Wallace and his Scottish army. Before the battle began, they sent

great victory. Never before had men fighting on their feet overthrown knights in armour. But in the battle, Andrew Murray was badly wounded. Soon afterwards, he died. Now Wallace was Guardian alone.

Still the man of action, he led his army into northern England. They destroyed towns and took back great quantities of plunder to Scotland. During all this time King Edward was away in France, fighting in another war. England was strong enough and rich enough to fight the French and the Scots at the same time, but Edward now decided it was time to deal with Scotland himself. He brought a great army up into the south of Scotland, although it was composed more of Welshmen and Irishmen than Englishmen. But the armoured knights, on their huge war-horses, were English.

Wallace did not advance to give battle. He knew that there was not enough food in the countryside for Edward's army to live on. He wanted to wait until the men were so tired and hungry that they would have to turn and go home. Then he would attack. His plan almost worked. Edward could not find Wallace's army. His men were running short of food and beginning to fight among themselves.

two friars to speak to
Wallace. They were
sure they would win
the battle. After all,
they had armoured
knights on horseback
and Wallace had only
foot-soldiers. The friars
gave Wallace a chance
to surrender without
fighting. Wallace sent
them back with this
defiant message:

"Go back and tell
your masters that we
come here not to ask
for peace as a boon (a
favour) but to fight for our freedom."

The battle began. Wallace's men were at one side
of the narrow bridge over the River Forth, the
English were on the other. To reach the Scots, the
English force had to cross the bridge. Wallace
waited for half of them to cross, then ordered his
men to attack. In a short time they had won. The
English commander fled away, and some of
Edward's hated governors were killed. It was a

But at last Edward, who still had Scottish helpers, managed to find out where Wallace had placed his army. The English army set off quickly to find it, and there was a long, hard battle at Falkirk. In the end, Edward won the day. Many Scots were killed, and Wallace had to hide in the forest.

The task of being Guardian was passed to another man, but Wallace did not give up his part in the fight for freedom. He went to France, where some of the lords and bishops of Scotland were living, to discuss with them what should be done next. He also went to Rome to see the Pope. Scotland had managed to get the Pope on her side, and it was hoped that he would be able to persuade Edward to leave Scotland and allow King John to return. When he returned to Scotland, Wallace again became a commander, no longer of a full-size army, because that was no longer possible, but of a small swift-moving band that could attack and disappear into the forest. In those days, there were still great forests covering much of Scotland.

Edward had hoped that his victory at Falkirk would make the Scots submit to him once more, but Wallace had shown that the English could be beaten. Others as well as Wallace kept up their attacks and raids. Each time the English took control of a castle, a band of Scots would appear out of nowhere and take it back. For more than a year this went on. Edward became more and more impatient. In the end he decided to crush all the resisters.

He returned to Scotland with another great army and organised a fleet of ships to bring food and fresh weapons for it. He marched up and down the country, capturing every castle that was held by the Scots until only Stirling Castle remained. When winter came, he did not go back to England but stayed in Dunfermline, the main home of the Scottish kings. In spring he would finish the job. This time it seemed as if his plan was working. Gradually, one after another, the Scottish lords who had fought against him came to make their submission.

The grim old king even received an offer of submission from William Wallace himself. Knowing that Edward hated him more than anyone, Wallace jokingly sent a message saying he would submit if Edward would promise him a plentiful supply of wood and cattle. But he knew that if he was ever captured Edward would show him no mercy. Edward believed that if it had not been for Wallace he would have been the master of Scotland years before.

Edward's reply was to offer a large reward to anyone who would bring him the head of Wallace. By now only one of Scotland's castles was not in Edward's hands. That was Stirling, set high on its rock, not far from the bridge where Wallace had won his great victory. The lion flag of the Scottish king still flew from its battlements. The English battered its walls with a huge machine called "Warwolf" and filled its moat with earth and stones. At last Stirling Castle too surrendered.

Edward was the master of Scotland, but his victory was not quite complete. One more thing would make it so – the capture of William Wallace.

As long as Wallace was free, the whole desperate struggle could start again. Wallace would never give up, even when every other leader in Scotland had surrendered. But while Wallace could escape the English, he could not escape his own people. For a year he continued the fight, now with only a tiny band of followers. But at last he was captured by Sir John of Menteith. This man, who handed Wallace over to the English, was seen as one of the greatest traitors in Scottish history, but he had sworn his loyalty to Edward, like every other important man in Scotland. He was only doing his duty. It is told that he did not actually say where Wallace was but simply turned over a loaf of bread on his table. This was the agreed signal to the English soldiers, who then went and took Wallace from Menteith's men.

Wallace was taken to London. Three weeks after his capture he was brought to trial in Westminster Hall. He was accused of treason against King Edward, his master. Treason was the crime of fighting against your own king. Wallace said that he was a loyal subject of the king of Scots and the

English had no right to accuse him of treason. Wallace had always loyally fought for his own king, John of Scotland. But Edward was determined to have his revenge against the man who had given him so much trouble. Defiant to the end, Wallace was brutally executed in London. He was alone, abandoned by his countrymen, in the power of his worst enemy, surrounded by the jeering London mob. That was on 23rd August in the year 1305.

Edward's victory now seemed complete. His control of Scotland was even stronger than when Wallace had first begun to fight back. But after Wallace's example, the Scottish people were not

24

prepared to submit meekly. Less than a year later, Robert Bruce, who had first supported Wallace then changed sides to help Edward, once again defied the power of Edward. He was crowned king of Scots in the ancient abbey of Scone. So the struggle went on for seven more years, until the Battle of Bannockburn ensured Scotland's independence. And William Wallace, the younger son of a country laird, who saved his country's honour in its darkest days, will not be forgotten as long as Scotland exists.

THE WALLACE STORY
AND WALLACE MONUMENTS

The great deeds of Wallace have been told by many people. One of the earliest was Blind Harry, a poet who lived in Scotland in the fifteenth century. He wrote a long poem, called simply *Wallace*, which was first recited at the court of King James the Fourth and became very popular. Blind Harry's poem was read and loved by Robert Burns, the greatest of Scottish poets. In our own time it inspired the film *Braveheart*, which tells Wallace's story.

Wallace was never forgotten, but it was not until the nineteenth century that people began to feel that there should be a special Wallace monument, which everyone could see, to help them remember what Wallace had done for Scotland.

In 1814 a great statue was set in position near Dryburgh, in a splendid position above the River Tweed. This statue is more than seven metres tall and was made for the Earl of Buchan by a local sculptor, John Smith. You can find the path to the

statue from the road between St Boswells and Dryburgh.

In 1821 a statue to Wallace was unveiled in the centre of Lanark, the town where his fight began. Then in 1869, the National Wallace Monument was completed on Abbey Craig, to the north of Stirling. To reach the top of this lofty tower, you have to climb 246 steps. Thousands of people from Scotland and all over the world sent money to help build it. Beside it is the Hall of Heroes, where you can find out more about Wallace and other heroes of Scotland.

There are monuments to Wallace in places outside Scotland as well. Baltimore, in the United States, has a copy of the statue on the National Monument, and there is another Wallace statue in Ballarat, Australia.

SOME DATES IN THE LIFE OF WILLIAM WALLACE

- ◆ Born around the year 1274

- ◆ Kills the sheriff of Lanark, 1297

- ◆ Battle of Stirling Bridge, 1297

- ◆ Battle of Falkirk, 1298

- ◆ Visit to France and Rome, 1299

- ◆ Returns to Scotland, 1303

- ◆ Captured, August 1305

- ◆ Executed in London, 23rd August 1305